FACTS

ON

RAISING

GAMEBIRDS

by Dianne Tumey
Harrah, Oklahoma

Table Of Contents

Basics of Good Gamebird Raising	5
Bobwhite Quail	6-8
Incubation	9
Suggested Brooding Schedule	13
Starting and Growing Chart	20
Water Medication	21
Debeaking	23
Humidity	24
Litter and Manure Management	24-25
Methods of Brooding	14
Coturnix Quail	26
Space Chart for Quail	32
Hatching Periods	39
Incubating Eggs In Small Quantities	40
Ventilation Of Incubators	42
Trouble-Shooting Your Hatch	45-46
Medications	47-48
Common Diseases	48-54
National Poultry Improvement Plan	55-59
Stress, Handling, Signs of Illness	61-62
Guineas	63
Junglefowl	64-65
Ringneck Pheasant	66-68
Chukar Partridge	71-73
If You Have Your Health	75-76
Fastrack - Probiotics	77
Predator Control	78
Internal Parasites	79-80
Cage Plans	83-89
Associations	90-91
Sources Of Equipment	92

The Five Basic Categories Of Good Gamebird Raising

1) **GENETICS**
2) **ENVIRONMENT**
3) **NUTRITION**
4) **SANITATION**
5) **DISEASE ANTICIPATION**

When raising gamebirds for commercial production or hobby it is essential to acquire your stock from is good reputable farm. Remember that you the owner are the key to the success in raising your gamebirds. Your commitment to the knowledge of the basics in good housing, nutrition, sanitation and preventive medicine are the most important first steps to years of success and good reputation.

Regardless of the numbers of gamebirds you keep or the purpose in raising them. The basics of good health remain the same.

 # Bobwhite Quail

Bobwhites are monogamous and usually pair off for life. This is why many breeders recommend individual cages to be the most successful and profitable method of producing Bobwhite Quail. However, we have tried both these methods and colony breeding in large flight pens to be just as successful although maintenance and sanitation is more difficult.

Eggs Production And Care

Normal mating season for Bobwhite Quail is mid May to mid August, during which time they may lay from 50 to 60 eggs in the wild. This can vary according to climate and weather conditions. Bobwhite Quail can be made to lay eggs the year round by providing at least 17 hours of light a day and a temperature above 60 degrees, and may produce 200 or more eggs per year. Breeders should be at least 6 months of age.

Eggs should be gathered daily and in hot weather, at least twice or more times. Hands should be clean and dry when handling eggs and should not be handled more than is absolutely necessary. It is believed to be best not to wash or wipe dirty eggs as you may remove the natural protective coating and seal the pores. We usually do wash our bobwhite quail and other gamebird eggs. We use plain Clorox mixed half and half with water and also a product called Tektrol and or Basic G (by Shakely Co.) . We use the Basic G mostly for the cleaning of the eggs because Tektrol is better suitable to be used for the cleaning of the incubators and other equipment. Tektrol can be absorbed through the skin and should be used with rubber gloves, but Basic G is not harmful in that way to you and excellent for the cleaning of the hatching eggs. Extremely dirty eggs should be discarded.

Eggs should be stored in cool, damp place if possible. A basement is an ideal place. But if you don't have one, keep the eggs in as cool a place as possible, but not in any drafts.

We store our eggs in an insulated room adjacent to our incubator room. We use a room air conditioner and run a commercial size egg room humidifier. Proper humidity in your egg room will prevent egg moisture loss. Our humidifier maintains 75 to 80% relative humidity in the average size egg room. It's quiet and extremely efficient, and uses less energy than a 75 watt light bulb. You can purchase one from a company called Farmtek. (Address in back of book)

Until time to go in the incubator the eggs must be turned daily to keep the yolk from settling to one side. You can lay the eggs on the side with the small end slightly lower and to turn, the eggs must be rolled all the way over. The best method of storing eggs is to use egg flats made especially for quail eggs. Eggs are placed in them with the small end straight down. Egg trays can then be placed in a box and the box propped up at a 45 degree angle. To turn the eggs, reverse the tilt angle so that they slant the other way. If you set the quail eggs within a seven day period this tilting is not necessary. Never store or set eggs with the large end down as the eggs will be ruined.

There are several containers that can be used for storing your eggs. Paper Mache containers are most commonly used but not as sanitary as plastic ones. If you used the paper Mache trays be sure to discard them if they become soiled. Plastic containers are ideal because they can be cleaned after each week of use and also sometimes you can store in them and then just place them in your incubator for setting , thus eliminating double work of unloading and loading them again for incubation.

GQF 3 TIERED INCUBATOR   GQF TABLETOP

HINT: Decide where to locate your incubator. Find a secluded area which is as undisturbed as possible, perhaps a basement room with minimal activity.

Incubation

Bobwhite Quail will not set on their eggs in captivity, so they must be set in an incubator. There are two types of incubators. 1. Still Air Incubators (operate anywhere from 100 1/2 degrees to 101F.) and 2. Circulated Air Incubators (operate at 99 1/2 degrees F.) During incubation eggs should be turned 3-5 times daily to prevent yolk from settling to one side and to exercise the embryo. It is recommended that eggs be turned during the first 70% of the incubation. You must accomplish this the best you can without disturbing the rest of the eggs occupying the incubator. In small table-top incubators it is difficult to maintain the correct temperatures if you are going and coming from it three or more times a day. Therefore, we recommend you only turn eggs twice a day if you do not have an automatic turner on your incubator. If you keep all the temperatures maintained you will have more success this way. If you have automatic turners, than set them for turning from three to four times daily.

Quail eggs would not be mixed with other types of eggs or eggs with different hatching times when it is time for them to hatch if it is possible not to. Bobwhite quail take from 23 to 25 days to hatch and turning of them should stop about the 20th day of incubation. Eggs are then placed on their side at that time and are no longer moved. The humidity is increased during the last few days before the hatch.

Remember:

· Plan ahead when determining the size and type of incubator to be used . Most game bird equipment companies can furnish you with capacities and capabilities of various makes and models.

- · If you plan on hatching and setting continuously you will need an incubator with a hatcher or a separate hatcher.

- · Keep a constant eye on your incubator and hatcher during operation to be sure the temperature and humidity are correct.

- · Your incubator and hatcher should be in a room where no major changes can occur in the temperature or humidity.

- · An incubator or brooder is designed to bring normal room temperature (70-degrees) up to the temperature and will not work properly in an unheated building in cold weather.

- To be successful, every game farm must have a good "Health Program" for their gamebirds. It's far better to prevent diseases than to try to cure them!

Brooding

When chicks are removed from the incubator they must have a place that is warm and dry. A brooder should have one section that is heated, with a temperature of 100 degrees (for the first week) and an unheated section for the feed and water and also so the birds may get away from heat if they get too hot. Temperature should be reduced 5 degrees each week until it is down to 70 degrees. Bobwhite Quail need a temperature around 70 degrees until they are about 12 weeks of age. By 16 weeks Bobwhite have their adult feathers and can endure freezing temperatures if they have been conditioned right. There are two basic types of brooding. The most common type is box type and floor type.

Box Type Brooders such as the 0402 from the G.Q.F. Company, which is ideal for small numbers of birds. These units are sturdy metal brooders that can hold up to 100 Bobwhite or just a few. You can purchase up to five and they can be stacked. This gives you more space and they also conserve heat when stacked and are portable.

Floor Brooding is cheaper but requires more room. Units such as the 0427, 0444, and 0445 can be placed over litter such as pine straw. The units use heat elements for heat rather than lights. Heat lamps can be used, but they heat small areas and are not controlled by a thermostat thus using more energy. Sometimes heat lamps can cause pecking problems because of the brightness of the light. There is also a Radiant Ray Brooder #0442, which runs on electricity. It can be purchased from G.Q.F. Company. Another excellent floor brooder is called a Hot Rock, it runs off of propane.

Feeding

Sanitation is very important at all times. Care should be taken that game birds do not eat musty feed from any source. The first feed for your baby quail should be hard boiled eggs finely chopped if you have some available. The eggs should be sprinkled over their gamebird starter.

The starter you use should be at least 28% protein. This feed should be placed near the birds in paper plates or on paper towels, so that they can find it easily without going far from the brooder heat for the first time for a few days. The boiled eggs are merely to help get the chicks started eating and prevent having some starve to death. This should be gradually discontinued by the 7th day.

WATER. Birds must have plenty of water at all times. For baby birds use a fruit jar waterier such a #4458 from G.Q.F., which is designed exclusively for quail and gamebirds to prevent drowning. This type drinker should be used for the first week in the brooder or longer. After this automatic drinkers may be used if so desired. Drinkers should be close to heated areas. If chicken waterier are used, put rocks or marbles in them to keep the chicks from getting wet or drowning. All baby birds should receive medication in their water for the first week along with a good vitamin electrolyte supplement. Solutracin 50 or Solutracin 200 and Terramycin are good preventive medications to use also. It is always a good idea to use a medication such as Terramycin when you have had baby chicks shipped into you. This will combat the stress of shipping.

Suggested Brooding Schedule

Preparation before removal from hatcher :

- Turn on all brooders and set at 100 degrees F.

- Place fresh water in all jars at end or side. (do not put in corner so that birds cannot crowd up around waterier)

- Place a flat container (such as paper plates etc.) for chicks to feed out of in more than one place in brooder.

- Do not use any container that is slick or birds can become straddle legged on slick surfaces.

- Make sure there are no drafts around brooder.

- Keep a close check on the temperature of all your brooders.

Be sure to cull weak or crippled birds from hatch.

METHODS OF BROODING

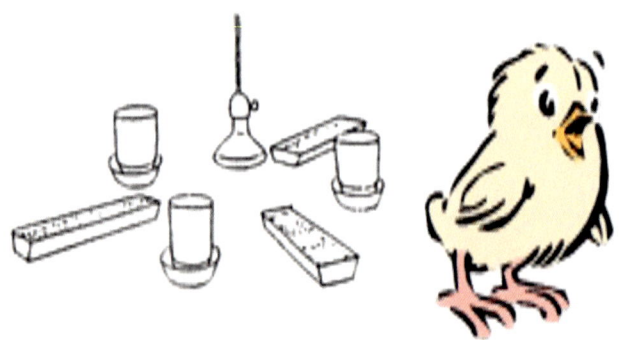

INFRA-RED BROODING LAMP

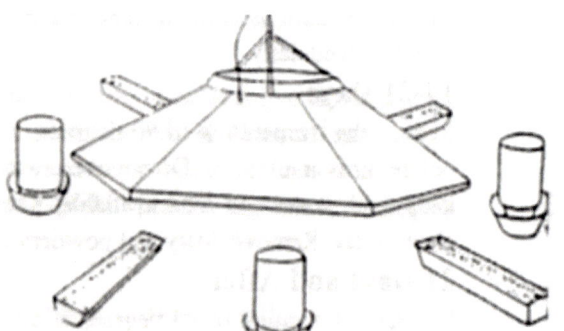

HOVER-TYPE BROODER

BATTERY-TYPE BROODER

1-7 Days

Always check brooders daily and nightly to be sure birds are comfortable. At this age they cannot stand fluctuating temperatures. Keep their waterier filled and cleaned daily. Remove any feed that has become contaminated with droppings. Place fresh feed out daily. Hard-boiled eggs is a good source of protein to grind up and sprinkle over the top of their grain. Just remember not to leave any that is not eaten within a few hours so as not to contaminate them. As the birds begin to eat better you can graduate them to a normal chick feeder.

7-14 Days

Reduce the temperature to 95 degrees. Continue to keep fresh water and feed available. Keep birds on a vitamin electrolyte administered in their water. Remove dusty and powdery feed daily.

14-21 Days

Reduce the temperature to 90 degrees. Keep feed and water before birds at all times. Do not overcrowd birds. Continue to keep fresh water and feed available. Keep birds on vitamin electrolytes. Remove dusty and powdery feed daily.

21 Days and After

Reduce temperature to 85 degrees and continue to reduce it each week thereafter. Continue sanitary procedures. Never fail to keep fresh water and feed out.

5-6 Weeks

Move to Grow Out Pens. If necessary cull and debeak as you move them.

Grow-Out

Depending on weather conditions you can usually place quail in grow-out pens by the age of 6 weeks.

Suggestions *For* Success

- Never overcrowd birds. Watch for signs of cannibalism and pecking.
- Be sure birds have plenty of feed and water stations.
- Placing water and feed on wire stands will reduce exposure to harmful organisms.
- Construct shelter and hiding places for protection from weather and from one another. We have shaded areas and also put out some cut cedar trees laid on the ground to provide the birds a place to feel secure.
- If growing birds for meat keep them on wire floors.
- · Pens that are on wire floors raised from the ground should have drop curtains around the bottom to prevent drafts.
- Be sure to have feed and water in front of birds at all times.
- Just observe them on a daily basis for any signs of health problems.
- Birds are usually released at 16 weeks of age.

_F_light _C_onditioning

Most hunting preserves request a strong, aggressive and fast flying bird. In order to achieve this with Bobwhite Quail you must condition them for at least 4 to 6 weeks. Some will want them as early as 12 weeks of age and others will want nothing but 16 week old birds. The following are a few points to remember when conditioning for flight birds.

- · Flight pens should have dirt floors, and be kept well drained. You can maintain flight pens above the ground on wire if you prefer.

- · Keep fresh water and feed out constantly.

· A flight pen should be at least 8 feet wide and 25 feet long. Do not overcrowd. Allow 2 sq.ft. per bird.

- · Make your pen easily accessible to a rototiller for turning the top soil after each group of birds leave.

- · Keeping feed and water on wire floors reduces birds exposure to organisms. The more natural a flight pen is, the better.

- · Use a top netting made for game birds to prevent any injuries to the birds when flying.

- · You should construct more than 1 flight pen to allow for rotating the various ages of birds. Only 1 person should have contact with birds.

- One person should have contact with the birds to allow for a more flighty bird. The more natural a flight pen is, the better.

Guide Incubator Settings Of Bobwhite Quail

Period of incubation………………………………23-25 days

Incubator (temperature at set)

Forced Air……………………………………………99 ½ F.

Still-Air……………………………………………100-101F.

At set………………………………………84-86 wet bulb

At pip………………………………………88-90 wet bulb

- It is usually important to follow the manufacturer's recommendation on temperature and humidity settings

- Problems with humidity is more common than with temperature. After a few hatches you might need to vary the settings from the manufacturer's guide for best results.

- For continuous incubation and where trays contain eggs of various stages of incubation, a commonly used temperature setting of 100 F. and a wet bulb reading of 90 degrees usually works satisfactorily.

Common Causes of Poor Hatchability In Bobwhite Quail

- Continual stress of breeders during mating season can cause a higher percentage of non-fertile eggs.
- Keeping your blood line over 3 years will result in problems.
- Setting eggs from old breeders.
- Males or females that are crippled or deformed can result in non-fertile eggs.
- Having too many females per male.
- Storing your hatching eggs too long before setting.
- Failure to turn eggs during incubation.
- Not allowing hatching eggs to reach room temperature before setting.
- Temperatures fluctuating during incubation a lot..
- Improper humidity during setting, at the end.
- Poor sanitation and failure to keep hatcher clean.
- Washing eggs improperly.

Starting & Growing Recommendations
Pheasants...............Growing Period

Age In Weeks	Feed	Lbs.
0-6	Starter	2.0
6-18 for meat	Grower	11.0
6-14 for release	Starter	6.5
14-18 for release	Grower	5.0
Total Feed	For Meat	13.0
	For Release	13.

Quail & Chukars
Growing................ Period

Age	Feed	Lbs.
0-6	Starter	1.5
6-12 for meat	Grower	4.5
6-8 for release	Grower	1.0
8-12 for release	Grower	4.0
Total Feed	For Meat	6.0
	For Release	6.5

Water Medication Is Important For Gamebirds

Disease outbreaks sometimes occur despite the best plans for prevention. When this happens, medication is usually needed quickly. Administering it in drinking water is a simple and quick method to get a small or large amount of birds medicated.

It is best to medicate only after obtaining an accurate, professional diagnosis. When administering drugs, to base this on a hunch can cause serious loss of time, can be counter-productive, and it is very expensive if you choose the wrong medication to use.

A good health program is designed to prevent the risk of disease and maintain a healthy flock continuously. When you have a disease outbreak it is not only expensive, but the need to medicate also complicates efforts to market residue-free birds.

The authority and responsibility associated with the administration of medication must be clearly understood by all persons involved. Medication can cause residues, and residues can result in product condemnation. Their use must be controlled and recorded. Only one person should administer medication that person should be responsible for the quantity used and duration.

Carefully read labels of all drugs used in water medication. They must follow the dosage level prescribed for the disease being treated. Never increase the dosage unless recommended by a veterinarian or other authority on drugs. Over medicating can causes death losses and deficiency in your birds.

Two basic methods are available for the water medication. A medication tank has a proportioner. The tank has the advantage of being very accurate when used properly. A known amount of the medication can be mixed in a known amount of water. Disadvantages are its size, unwieldiness, and difficulty to keep clean.

There are several proportioners on the market. These work on the principle of water flow, providing either a siphoning effect or pumping action to meter out a drug. These units are small and portable, and sometimes not very accurate. They should be monitored several times a day.

Drugs must be very soluble in order to dissolve in the concentrated stock solution being proportioned into the water, which is usually one ounce per gallon of water.

The correct delivery of water medication is based on water consumption. Using an average figure, one accepts that some birds drink more than others, so extremely sick and depressed birds may not be properly treated. You must also consider the factors of environmental temperature, palatability of medication, electrolyte intake, and condition of the flock. On a hot day, water consumption is increased resulting in over medication. Depressed birds drink very little and will be under medicated.

Some medications may actually promote bacterial growth in the water (especially in hot weather). waterier should be cleaned at least twice during the medication period. After medication has passed through water lines, rinse the lines (with a disinfectant solution if the medication used contain sugar) to remove the medication. Rinse proportioners and/or tanks three times after use. Invert and dry tanks until needed again.

Debeaking

Debeaking is the clipping off of some of the upper beak to prevent feather picking and injury to other quail. This is often done when birds are crowded in brooders and pens. Usually you should debeak during the first week in the brooding stage, and than again when they are about 6 to 8 weeks of age. Hand clippers are easy to use and do the job well. If you are raising large numbers of gamebirds you may find an electric debeaker to be easier to use. An electric debeaker will cut and burn through the beak which kills germs, helps stop bleeding, and does not crush the beak. You should exercise great care to prevent debeaking too severely. Hunting preserves do not generally like debeaked birds.

 ## *Humidity*

The panting rate of gamebirds is affected by high humidity. The higher the humidity is, the more rapid the respiration. Because the air is moist, it cannot absorb as much moisture from the lungs of a panting gamebird. Therefore, the bird must pant even faster.

When a gamebird chick is exposed to both high humidity and high temperature its unable to pant fast enough to dissipate body heat. When this occurs, death usually follows. Provide good draft-free air circulation, to reduce humidity. Regardless of the bird's age, they cannot tolerate both high temperatures and high humidity.

Litter and Manure Management

All gamebird producers want to provide the best environmental conditions in the housing of their flocks. One of the most important considerations is good manure management. Producers using wire floors eliminate many of the problems associated with poor manure conditions. The manure can be easily scraped or washed out of the house, thus eliminating potential disease and fowl air problems. When birds are raised on the ground this proposes a different problem. They are in constant contact with the manure and subject to all the hazards that come along with it. The important considerations is to select the right kind of litter. Many different materials have been used for litter, but the material selected is largely dependent on what is locally available. The two most common litter materials used in most areas are pine shavings and clean sand. (small chicks will eat sand and not feed—Do Not Use Sand on Chicks!) Other materials often used include straw, rice or peanut hulls untreated), corn cobs, shredded cane stalks, and cotton seed hulls (untreated). Pine shavings are usually considered the best litter material available. It has excellent handling qualities, and is inexpensive. Hardwood shavings are not as desirable because they can promote fungal growth that leads to aspergillosis (brooder pneumonia). Clean sand is popular but lacks cushioning, insulating, and water absorption.

The important thing to remember is always keep litter dry. Litter conditions influence bird performance, which in turn affects profits of growers. Dry litter helps control ammonia levels, provides a healthy flock environment and reduces condemnations due to hock and footpad burns.

Adequate ventilation will achieve this goal, so don't skimp on the air, even when birds are small. It's less expensive to burn a little extra gas early to maintain dry litter than to fight ammonia and wet litter and the negative consequences associated with them throughout the flock.

Advise: Today, frequent use of built-up litter requires greater attention to detail than every before. Gamebird litter consists of bedding material (shavings, rice hulls etc.)., manure, feathers, and other components. Dry litter is important for the health and welfare of birds, as well as the people who work in the housing areas of the birds.

Coturnix Quail

Housing The Quail

The Coturnix is a fast growing bird that is mature in six weeks of age and will start laying eggs at 6 to 7 weeks. It is therefore ideal for production as meat bird, however as well. They can be raised in a minimum of expense and care. For the beginner raiser this is an excellent quail to learn all about gamebird raising.

Some of the information for raising Bobwhite quail is ideal for the production of Coturnix. Read and follow instructions for raising Bobwhite Quail. The following information gives more specifics relating to the Coturnix.

Coturnix Quail may be kept in any form of cage that will keep them from flying out. Many of your chicken farms have surplus cages, brooders and other equipment suitable for keeping quail. Birds may be keep in large or small colonies on wire, concrete, or earth floors. About 50 square inches is ample floor space for each producing bird, and any height over 7 inches is ample head room. Quail may lay a bit better on wire in enclosures no larger than 3 ft. wide and 6 ft. long. Such space is provided in chick brooders with the heaters removed. Unused tiered brooders usually can be obtained at very small cost from chicken farmers who no longer need them. These make the finest type of colony cages for laying developing and growing quail. Homemade cages of similar construction are simple to make.

Coturnix Quail do not "pair off", therefore one cock can serve two hens. Colony breeding units are normally setup on the basis of one cock per two hens. Colony breeding is a method used quite frequently. For fertile eggs, forty hens and 20 cocks may be kept on a floor 3 ft. by 6 ft. or therefore, if eggs are not used for hatching, but for food, 60 laying hens may be kept in the same area making it possible to get up to 300 eggs per day out of a 5 tiered cage, such as converted chicken brooder.

The Coturnix Quail are so easy to raise rarely having any problem with diseases or cannibalism. The Universities report the Coturnix is generally more resistant to diseases than chickens and all gamebirds. Eggs hatch in 16 to 17 days and percentages of fertility are as high as with the best of poultry birds. There is little loss in growing birds.

Closely caged growing birds or laying birds will be gentle natured causing a commotion when being fed, inspected or handled. Yet, these same gentle natured caged birds will revert to the wild quickly. Birds penned in large flight cages will develop strong wings in three days to a week and will respond quickly in flight. Birds taken from exercising cage will fly like wild birds when released on a hunting range.

*F*eeding

Coturnix breeders require a feed containing 17 to 21% protein (chicks require an even h higher percentage). Such levels can be found in commercial turkey starter and gamebird starter, but if you can't get these you can use a feed with less protein and supplement it with grain, sprouts, and bugs. (A small light in or near the cage will attract insects to your birds "dinner table".) We have found the best feeds are ACCO, A&M, and Purina.

These are different levels of nutrition needed for gamebirds during the normal stages of its life. Generally you need to feed a protein level of 27% to 30% for chicks up to 6 weeks of age, switching to 20% for growing birds and 21% for meat birds and as I stated before 17%-21% for breeders.

*B*reeding

The quail begin to breed and lay eggs at only 6 to 8 weeks of age.......as opposed to the 20-24 weeks required for a chicken and 24-26 weeks for a Bobwhite Quail to begin producing. You should use the best looking birds for breeding of course. Two of the six breeds of Coturnix can be sexed by color at about three weeks. Both males of the Australian Fawn and the Pharoah have brick red breasts, where as the females breasts are speckled. The Australian Speckled Fawn males have a brick red color on their head and neck, but the female is buff color with dark speckles all over. The other breeds must be sexed by vent examination after they have begun to breed because they are the same color. A sexually active male will have a rounded protrusion above his vent. When this ball is gently squeezed a "foam" will run out. (the foam, which resembles shaving cream, is a kidney discharge). The size of the ball indicates the degree of interest the male has in mating. The breeding ratio can be one male two females or simply one to one. The best way is to put each pair or trio in a separate pen. A higher fertility rate is obtained this way in most cases.

The laying cycles of Coturnix are like those of many other types of poultry keyed to the increase and decrease of their daylight. The birds improve their productivity when the days start to lengthen in early spring, lay well as long as daylight lasts 17 hours or more, and then slows down. This means that, at the end of September, you must provide extra light if you want to prolong the period of good production. You can use a 60 watt bulb for every two-tiered chicken brooder or similar good cage…..or if you prefer install individual bulbs of say 7 to 15 watts in each coop.

*S*etting and *H*atching *I*nstructions

Domestic quail have lost the brooding instinct, thus their eggs must be hatched artificially. When using an incubator, never assume that you already know how to use the product…..make sure to read the manufacture's instructions carefully. After this, allow the incubator to run for 2 or 3 days before putting any eggs in it. Once they are in the incubator make sure to turn them every morning and evening, unless you have an automatic turning incubator, if you do it will do the turning for you and you have to check on the temperature of the incubator each day. Quail eggs should be set at 99.5 degrees F. Eggs should be place small end down and turned 90 degrees three times a day. On the 17th—18th day eggs should hatch. Always resist the temptation to help weak chicks usually (if they survive) grow into sickly and inferior adult quail. The ones that do peck their way successfully into the world should be allowed to fluff and dry out well before being put into a brooder.

If eggs are to be held any length of time before they are set, they should be kept small end down, turned three times a day and kept at a temperature of 60-68 degrees F.

Always be sure your hands are free of dirty and grease when handling eggs. Remember to always clean your incubator thoroughly after each hatch.

***B*rooding *I*nstructions**

Review the Bobwhite Quail instructions for incubators and brooding. The main difference with Coturnix eggs is that they should hatch in 17 days instead of 23 for Bobwhite. Day old birds should be kept at 95 degrees F. the first week and dropped 10 degrees each week there after until no heat is needed. Coturnix will generally not need any heat after the sixth week because of the maturity. Feed and water should be kept at random around brooder to insure birds get started drinking and eating. Flat lids from egg cartons make good feeders the first week. (If waterers are not designed for gamebird chicks, marbles or washed gravel may be placed in waterer to prevent chicks from getting wet or drowning.) Avoid all corners where chicks might pack up. If you have any kind of light bulb in your incubator be sure it is either red or green. (we just spray one with red) Bright light at this age causes pecking and cannibalism. Most feed dealers carry some type of gamebird starter.

All gamebirds require a good high protein feed. We recommend Acco, A&M or Purina. (It is all 28.5% protein) We also litter our baby quail for one week on straw poult pads. (if this is not available to you, use pine wood shavings or cottonseed hulls) Do not use cedar shaving as it irritates their eyes and also be careful that the cottonseed hulls you get are clean and not treated. Remember to remove them from litter after one week.

This gives them time to build their strength and coordination and also keeps drafts from chilling them when they are brooded on wire.

MORE HELPFUL HINTS!

- If you get chicks shipped in try using a tablespoon of sugar to a quart of water the first 24 hours after you receive them. This will make them thirsty and they will drink readily—thus you will prevent dehydration that sometimes can occur when birds are shipped.

- 1/4 " hardware cloth is too small to use on the floor of breeder age quail because the droppings will not fall through. Most breeders use 1/2 " hardware cloth so the floor area where the birds will be housed will remain much cleaner.

- In order to control disease you should best try to prevent it first.

APPROXIMATE SPACE NEEDED FOR QUAIL

	1-10 DAYS	10 DAYS-6WKS.	6 WKS.
FLOOR	6 BIRDS	4 BIRDS	2 BIRDS
	per sq.ft.	per sq.ft.	per sq.ft.
FEEDER	1/2"	1"	1 1/2"
	Per bird	per bird	per bird
WATER	0.25 "	0.25"	0.3"
	Per bird	per bird	per bird

Meat Bird Production

Although Coturnix are mature after 6 weeks, they have not reached their full body weight until after 10 weeks. Temporary caponization of Coturnix by light denial will create a much larger and fatter bird. Light Denial decreases the sex urge and egg production. This most desirable light denial can be handled in one of two ways. The birds may placed in a completely darkened room and have a time turn lights on for 8 hours each day or they may be raised in a very low or dim lighting. To reverse this temporary caponization, just return birds to normal lighting for 10 days.

Breeds of Coturnix Quail

Pharoah XLD1. The Pharoah is the gamebird of Europe and Asia. It is splendid for release on the American hunting range or as a dog training bird. It does well released in any climate, the humid tropics, the scorching deserts or snowclad landscapes. They are by far the largest strain available. Starting to lay at six weeks, it lays almost everyday of the year. They lay the big eggs that are eaten by the Asiatic peoples and a splendid gourmet item on the menu of other races. Everyone considering quail raising as a business or hobby should start with this strain as the principle breed for laying birds.

Tibetan. The Tibetan are fast flying, flush well and most of all they are aggressive. Their color is a rich dark brown with stripes on the back and gray and white feathering in the head. The male and female are both colored alike but the female is a little larger than the male in size. These quail are highly immune to most diseases that other quail such as the Bobwhite get. They are hardy and disease free birds as all the Coturnix are. They withstand the hottest and coldest of temperatures and can be as good as a Bobwhite quail if you raise them the same and give them a chance. They can be ready for training or hunting as early as 8 to 10 weeks of age and of course are already laying eggs by the time they are 6 to 7 weeks of age. Through careful management and selective breeding we have developed this fine breed to be in demand as much as the Bobwhite and Pharoah. **British Range.** Actually it is difficult to describe the exact color of this beautiful quail. It has been called black. It has been called blue. It is definitely a rich dark colored bird, but with gun metal glintings edging the feathers. At a distance, it appears to be a solid black. Closer viewing shows the glinting tints of brown gun metal intermingled throughout producing an aristocratic color tone. It is a mutation of the best Coturnix laying strains produced in the British Isles. It is a fine, colorful bird for release on the hunting range as well as a great layer of large eggs. It has all the fast producing and much of the fast growth of the Pharoah. The size of the British Range is not up to standard of the Pharoah however, fine bird it is, and will do well on the hunting range, as well as be an excellent producer of eggs for food or hatching. **English White.** The English White is the final answer to the demand for a pure white quail with good eyesight. The English White is an English imported mutation. It lays generally in 7 weeks and matures slightly slower than the Pharoah D1 reaching its full growth by 8 weeks of age. The English White is the kind of quail everyone has been looking for. It is not an albino because it has dark eyes and therefore can see well in the sun and bright lights. Because the eyes are normally pigmented, the English White see as well as any quail and may be released on the h hunting range, if so desired. This quail has all the vitality of the colored Coturnix quails. Hatching percentages of eggs are high, mortality of growing chicks is low and grown birds are fully as active and strong as other strains of Coturnix. The English White quail seems to have some advantage over the other strains as a warm climate producer of eggs laying best in hot, humid climate. **Tuxedo.** The Tuxedo quail comes to you decked out in black coat and white shirts, as it were. This bird is not only a real beauty of a quail, but one that lays just as well and grows as fast as any of the Coturnix quails. The two-color scheme of this bird would make it an easy bird to spot on the hunting range. It retains all the fine qualities of the best nd fast laying Coturnix species.

Australian Speckled Fawn. The Fawn is a beautiful buff color with the males having a brick red color on their head and neck, and the female is buff color with dark speckled all over. It lays generally in 7 weeks and matures slightly slower as does the English White. This Coturnix variety is very popular for its' beauty. When fully mature it turns out to be very close to the large size of the

Pharoah D1 and an excellent egg layer as well.

You Get Quick Results With Coturnix Quail!!!

All the Coturnix quails give you quick results. You do not wear your patience out waiting for them to "come season". There is no season on the Coturnix quails. The lay every day of the year regardless of the severity of the weather. You can easily get four generations and possibly FIVE GENERATIONS of Coturnix while you are waiting for the American quail to lay their first egg!!!!!

More Helpful Hints

- It is a good practice to put this medicine in the water five to six days after and before moving birds or anytime they are under stress of any kind also. We use Vitamin Electrolytes and Fastrack.

- Don't use large mesh wire when you are constructing quail pens because the birds can get their heads caught and then strangle.

- Contain ground pens—Use bricks, cement blocks, or a platform constructed of wood and hardware cloth to elevate water levels so that the drinking surface isn't filled with dirt when the birds scratch.

- Daily observation of your birds is important for you to readily notice changes in their behavior.

- Don't feed laying rations to chicks. Too much calcium is harmful to the growth and development of chicks. Chicks which are four or five weeks old require only about 1% calcium in their diet.

- Vitamin E is a critical vitamin in the diet of gamebirds. Gamebird rations contain sufficient rations of vitamin E, but if the feed is old or was stored in a warm humid place, the feed could be low in both vitamin E and vitamin A. Vitamin E deficiency can cause male birds to become permanently sterile and unable to fertilize eggs. Hens which are deprived of

- vitamin E will continue to lay eggs, but will be produce inferior chicks. It can cause death in breeders fed a diet deficient in vitamin E. Natural sources of vitamin E are wheat, Niger and sunflower seeds, and greens. Birds cannot assimilate vitamin E without the trace mineral Selenium.

- 1/4" hardware cloth is too small to use on the floor of breeder age quail because the droppings will not fall through. Most breeders use 1/2" hardware cloth so the floor area where the birds will be housed will remain much cleaner.

To maintain strong egg shells toward the end of the laying cycle in late June through August, lightly top dress the feed of gamebirds two times a week with pellet sized oyster shells.

*H*atching *P*eriods

Eggs held longer in a storage require slightly longer hatching times. This is why some game farms set the older eggs ten hours sooner than the fresher hatching eggs. Hatching eggs are best stored in cooler areas operated at 55 degrees F. and 75% relative humidity. Most large scale commercial game farms set eggs every 7 days. This produces a weekly hatching and shipping schedule. Eggs held longer than 10 days produce a much lower percentage of hatch-ability.

	DAYS
COTURNIX QUAIL	17-18
BOBWHITE QUAIL	23-24
BUTTON QUAIL	15-16
RINGNECK PHEASANTS	21-25
CHUKAR PARTRIDGE	22-23
GUINEA FOWL	26-28
TURKEY	28
PRAIRIE CHICKEN	25-36
DOMESTIC CHICKEN	21
GAMBEL QUAIL	24
RUFFLED GROUSE	23
HUGARIAN PARTRIDGE	24
RHEA	42
OSTRICH	42
JUNGLEFOWL	21
SWAN	42
GEESE	28-32
PEKING DUCK	28
MUSCOVY DUCK	33-37
PEAFOWL	28
PIGEONS	16-18

Incubating Eggs In Small Quantities

Once you have selected the type of poultry you wish to raise, you must then purchase your eggs from a reputable, licensed hatchery. Dealing with a licensed hatchery will insure you get healthy chicks from tested stock. The National Poultry Improvement Plan will be glad to issue you a list of your state hatchery and individual participants. The next step is to choose your incubator. Be sure that the incubator you use provides controlled conditions. You may want to have one that has a viewing window so that you can observe the whole process.

Sometimes we overlook the fact that you can use natures best incubator the brood hen. A broody hen can cover about 12 to 14 chicken eggs, 9 to 11 duck eggs, or 4 to 6 goose eggs. (Pheasant and chukar eggs are comparable to a bantam chicken egg.) General purpose breeds like New Hampshire and Plymouth Rocks and Japanese Silkies Bantams make better setters than breeds such as the leghorn.

Be sure to keep a good eye on the temperature and humidity during incubation. The follows a chart to go by for various types of poultry.

Remember To Clean Your Incubator

Thoroughly After Each Hatch!

TEMPERATURE	TYPE OF INCUBATOR	HUMIDITY
99 1/2 F. - 99 3/4 F.	FORCED AIR	82-86% wet bulb
100 F. - 101 F.	STILL AIR	50-52% relative

*T*urning

Quail eggs do not necessarily need to be turned before incubation, but once set should be turned from 2-5 times a day. chicken, Chukar, Pheasant, Turkey, Duck, Goose, Peacock, or any exotic pheasant eggs must be turned prior to setting at least 2 times a day and after incubation from 2-5 times a day. They should be turned until three days before hatching time.

Of course, in commercial operations the incubators are always automatic and when the turning process is in effect there is no harm to altering the temperature or humidity of the incubation. But when you are using a small table-top incubator this process if not done quickly can alter the temperature and humidity of the incubator and thus would effect the hatchability of your eggs. So be careful to get the job done as quickly as you can so as not to chill the eggs to often during the incubation time.

*V*entilation *Of I*ncubators

Your incubator is usually equipped with vents to permit a slow change of air. Little ventilation is needed when incubation starts; it may be increased gradually as incubation progresses. During hatching, restrict ventilation in order to raise the humidity.

Shoving an incubator up against a wall or placing equipment on both sides of the incubator restricts the air flow. High levels of carbon dioxide will cause slow development of the embryos, increased changes of abnormalities, weak chicks, and reduced hatchability.

*H*int*:* If bits of shell stick to newly hatched chicks, this is due to the humidity being to low.

<u>The chart on the following page is adapted from material produced by the Cooperative Extension Service, Clemson University, and is offered as a guide only. Follow the specific instructions of your manufacturer for best results.</u>

<u>*For The Best Hatches*</u>

<u>*Know Your Procedures*!!</u>

Chicken	Turkey	Duck	Muscovy	Goose	Guinea	Pheasant	Peafowl	Bobwhite	Coturnix	Chukar
21	28	28	35-37	28-34	28	23-25	28-30	23-25	17-18	23-25
99.75	99.25	99.5	99.5	99.25	99.75	99.5	99.25	99.5	99.5	99.5
85-87	83-85	84-86	84-86	86-88	83-85	86-88	83-85	84-86	84-86	80-82
99	98.5	98.75	98.75	98.5	99	99	98.5	99	99	99
18th day	25th day	25th day	31st day	25th day	25th day	21st day	25th day	20th day	14th day	20th day
86-88	82-84	90-94	90-94	90-94	80-82	82-84	82-84	88-90	86-88	80-82

INCUBATION TEMPERATURES & HUMIDITY

Wet Bulb reading is read with hygrometer. The chart above show Wet Bulb readings.

The forced air incubator should use a wet bulb reading. Wet bulb readings cannot be used with a still-air incubator. Still-air incubators use a relative reading.

Relative Humidity is read with a Barometer.

Still-air incubators should use a temperature of 100-101 degrees when setting. Relative humidity should be used to read the humidity for a still-air incubator. 50% Relative humidity = 83 degrees wet bulb. Still-air s must use a relative reading for the humidity to be correct.

Use Hygrometers to read wet bulb.

Use Barometers to read relative humidity.

You purchase hygrometers or barometers from the following companies: Thermometer and Thermometer/hygrometers from:

Cutlers Supply .www.cutlersupply.com .

Barometers can be bought at most Lowes Stores. An outdoor/indoor barometer can be used possibly.

Trouble-Shooting To Determine Factors Affecting The Hatch

Condition of Eggs

1. No embryonic development
2. Eggs showing a blood ring
3. Dead embryos during first week
4. Fully developed chicks, but dead without pipping
5. Chicks pipped but dead in shell
6. Chicks pipped and stuck in shell, shells are dry.
7. Sticky chicks, appear wet or are covered with contents of egg.
8. Chicks hatch early, may have bloody navels or rough navels.
9. Weak chicks
10. Short down on chicks
11. Small chicks
12. Large, soft-bodied chicks, dead chicks on trays, bad odor
13. Delayed hatch, chicks pipping more than three days later than should
14. Prolonged hatch, few chicks
15. Malformed chicks in good hatch
16. Malformed chicks in poor hatch

Probable Causes

Infertile Eggs Due To—

1. Sterile males
2. High degree or inbreeding
3. Too few; too many males
4. Inadequate nutrition; insufficient water.
5. Weather conditions
6. Seasonal decline toward end of breeding season
7. Birds too crowded

Improper Care Of Eggs—

1. Excessive chilling or heating or egg
2. Eggs held too long
3. Eggs held under improper temp. and humidity

REMEMBER TO CLEAN YOUR

INCUBATOR

THOROUGHLY AFTER EACH HATCH!!!

Other Causes

1. Improper fumigation of incubator

2. Improper nutrition of breeders

3. Mishandling of eggs during shipment

4. Disease problems or inbreeding

5. Improper turning of eggs

6. Power Failure

7. Infected eggs, usually from dirty eggs being sent.

8. Low humidity

9. Improper gathering of eggs

Medications

The following medications are recommended to keep on hand any disease outbreak that you might encounter when raising these quail or any gamebirds.

1. **Aureomycin Soluble Powder** for colds, coryza, air sac, & enteritis.

2. **Terramycin Soluble Powder** for all respiratory problems.

3. **Gallimycin Soluble Powder** for hard to cure respiratory and enteritis and also good for coryza.

4. **Solutracin-200 Soluble Powder** for bacterial enteritis and air sac.

5. **Sulmet Liquid** for infectious coryza, coccidiosis, pullorum, etc.

6. **Vita-Start Vitamins** for body building and stress.

Most Common Diseases

When raising all gamebirds it is advisable that the best medicine is preventive medicine. As a preventive to disease you should give them vita-start to keep their bodies strong and healthy. It is a vitamin electrolyte supplement. There are other brands of this available at most feed stores. Use whatever is sold by your local feed store. The following is a description of some common diseases you may encounter.

*Ul*cerative *E*nteritis (Quail Disease)

This is the most common and destructive disease of quail in many areas. Losses in young birds may reach 100 percent if not controlled. It is most commonly seen in ground or litter-reared quail, but may also occur in wire-reared birds. It is thought to be caused by a bacterium found in the intestinal tract. Individual birds can contact the disease organisms over a period of time on infected premises, and some mortality may occur almost continuously. You can identify ulcerative enteritis yourself by opening a sick or dead bird. Usually you will readily see ulcers on the intestines of the bird. Secondary infections may also be present which you cannot identify; thus the laboratory examination is still the best and most accurate. Contact your veterinarian to precede with this method. Disease is usually transmitted by ingesting contaminated droppings. Recovered birds may still be carriers of the organisms and a source of infection for non-infected birds. Isolate known infected stock from non-infected birds. Isolate known infected stock from non-infected stock. Pens, cages, and particularly ground or litter runs may remain infected over a long period of time. Thorough cleanup of premises is essential to prevention. Raising birds on wire is usually effective in helping to prevent the problem, but it is no guarantee the birds will not get it. Treatments vary in effectiveness according to management and sanitation that is practiced on your farm. If medication is necessary, we recommend Solutracin 50 or Solutracin 200.

Preventing this disease is more economical than curing it. Follow general recommended tips for disease prevention and hopefully you will never experience it or at least be able to control the spread of it. Keep up with changing times and situations.

Chronic Respiratory Disease
(Air Sac Disease)

Chronic Respiratory Disease (CRD), air sac syndrome and infectious sinusitis of turkeys have a common cause. CRD was recognized first as causing a chronic but mild disease in adult chickens. It reduced egg production but caused little or no mortality. After CRD had been recognized, a condition known as "air sac disease" became a problem in young birds. It caused high mortality in some flocks. Many birds became stunted; there was poor feed efficiency, and many were rejected as unfit for human consumption when processed.

The third condition, infectious sinusitis in turkeys, was recognized as early as 1906. It causes a sinus swelling under the eye as well as an inflammation of respiratory organs. It is a chronic disease adversely affecting growth and feed conversion which may cause significant mortality in young poults.

Uncomplicated CRD produces slight respiratory symptoms such as coughing, sneezing and a nasal discharge. In the air sac syndrome there is an extensive involvement of the entire respiratory system. The air sacs often are cloudy and contain large amounts of exudate. Three is often a film of exudate covering the liver, as well as the heart muscle and heart sac. Affected birds become droopy, feed consumption decreases and there is a rapid loss of body weight.

Infectious sinusitis in turkeys occurs in two forms. When the "upper" form is present, there is only a swelling of the sinus under the eye. In the "lower" form, the lungs and air sacs are involved. The air sacs become cloudy and may contain large amounts of exudate. Both forms of the disease usually are present in the flock and frequently are present in the same bird.

All gamebirds are subject to this disease as any turkeys or chickens are susceptible. It will often occur in Bobwhite quail around the age of two to three weeks of age in the lower form. When this occurs it is usually caused from the temperature not being regulated and the birds getting hot and cold to quickly.

Diagnosis of either of these conditions must be based on flock history, symptoms and lesions. Blood tests are useful in determining whether a flock is infected. If these symptoms occur in your flock and large numbers of mortality occurs have your birds tested by a vet immediately.

Infectious sinusitis in turkeys occurs in two forms. When the "upper" form is present, there is only a swelling of the sinus under the eye. In the "lower" form, the lungs and air sacs are involved. The air sacs become cloudy and may contain large amounts of exudate. Both forms of the disease usually are present in the flock and frequently are present in the same bird.

All gamebirds are subject to this disease as any turkeys or chickens are susceptible. It will often occur in Bobwhite quail around the age of two to three weeks of age in the lower form. When this occurs it is usually caused from the temperature not being regulated and the birds getting hot and cold to quickly.

Diagnosis of either of these conditions must be based on flock history, symptoms and lesions. Blood tests are useful in determining whether a flock is infected. If these symptoms occur in your flock and large numbers of mortality occurs have your birds tested by a vet immediately.

Many antibiotics have been used with varying success. Whether to give treatment is a decision that must be based on economic factors. If treatment is attempted, give high levels of one of the broad spectrum antibiotics either in the feed, drinking water or by injections. The "upper" form of infectious sinusitis has been treated with success by injecting antibiotics direct into the swollen sinus. Two widely used medications for this disease are Aueromycin and Gallimycin soluble powder administered in the water.

<u>Coccidiosis</u>

.Coccidiosis is a protozoan disease of fowl characterized by diarrhea, unthriftiness and variable mortality. It is a problem in all poultry—producing areas. Despite recent advances in control and treatment, the disease remains one of the principal causes of economic loss to the poultry industry.

Coccidiosis is caused by minute, microscopic animals called coccidian. There are a number of species of coccidian, each of which produces a distinct disease process. Coccidiosis is transmitted by direct or indirect contact with droppings of infected birds.

Coccidia are extremely hardy and may survive long periods outside the bird's body. They are transmitted easily from one house or premise to another by transmitted easily from one hour or premise to another by such things dirty boots, free flying birds, feed sacks and equipment.

Signs of a coccidiosis outbreak usually are general. Affected birds become pale and droopy, tend to huddle, consume less feed and water, have diarrhea and may become emaciated and dehydrated. Laying birds will experience a drop in production.

It is difficult, if not impossible, to prevent coccidiosis by sanitation practices alone. Coccidiosis is prevented best by feeding a coccidiostat, a drug added to feed at low levels and fed continuously. A good coccidiostat should:

- Prevent clinical outbreaks of coccidiosis.
- Have no undesirable side effects.
- Allow a natural immunity to coccidiosis to develop in the flock if exposure is present.
- Be inexpensive.

' A coccidiosis vaccine available commercially is useful in certain types of operations but it should not be used indiscriminately. Seek expert advice before using the vaccine.

Selection of drugs which are quite effective for treating coccidiosis is dependent upon many factors including withdrawal regulations toxicity problems, species involved and other disease conditions.

Remember: To be successful, every game farm must have a good "Health Program" for their gamebirds. It's far better to prevent diseases than try to cure them!

New Pigeon Disease Possible Threat To Poultry Industry

A relatively new pigeon disease, *which spread rapidly throughout Europe between 1981 and 1983 and was diagnosed in New York in 1985, may pose a threat to the commercial poultry industry.

The disease, which is caused by the same type of virus that causes Newcastle Disease, affects both racing pigeons and free (wild) pigeons. It differs from Newcastle, however, in that it can be transmitted from one pigeon to another as well as from pigeons to chickens. This means that any outbreak in pigeons anywhere is a possible threat to the commercial poultry or gamebird industry. Another difference is that once chickens are affected, the virulence of the disease increases as it passes from one chicken to another.

Because the structure of this virus differs slightly from that found in cases of Newcastle, it is uncertain whether chickens vaccinated for Newcastle can develop sufficient antibodies against the pigeon disease. The present assumption is that sufficiently NDV-vaccinated and immunized chickens will also be protected against the pigeon disease.

Just to be on the safe side, producers should keep all pigeons away from poultry houses; refrain from keeping any kinds of pigeons; stay away from all pigeons, especially racing pigeons; submit sick or dead pigeons to diagnostic lab; follow a sound vaccination program and regularly monitor the success of Newcastle vaccination programs, and maintain a rigid farm bio-security system. With these precautions in place, there is no need for undue concern - Poultry Post, Volume I, Number VIII March 1985.

National Poultry Improvement Plan

Pullorum is a bacterial disease of poultry that is transmitted from a hen to her chicks via the egg. By testing adult birds and eliminating disease carriers from the breeding flock, commercial chicken and turkey raisers have eliminated this costly disease. The fact is, it has been so long since most people have seen pullorum that it comes as sort of a shock to learn that it is still around. But pullorum can be found in small breeding flocks of fancy, poultry and sometimes gamebirds.

The National Poultry Improvement Plan, NPIP, was started in the early 1930's to coordinate State programs aimed at elimination of pullorum from commercial poultry. In those days, there were many poultry breeders serving the needs of thousands of small flock owners. Today, there are only a very few breeders of commercial poultry to serve the commercial raisers of flocks, which may number into the millions.

The only small breeders left are those that raise fancy fowl. Some 2,500 of these breeders, and hatcheries that deal in fancy fowl, are members of NPIP. A list of these pullorum-clean members is available from the NPIP staff, so everyone can find out where to buy clean stock.

The plan is administered by the U.S. Department of Agriculture, which maintains a small staff at the Agricultural Research Center, Beltsville, Md., to service the needs of NPIP. The Plan is a voluntary program conducted by State agencies and cooperating poultry industry segments.

In many states, pullorum-testing is a free service provided by the official state agency. In other states, there is small charge. In many states, it is possible to get training so individual poultry raisers can conduct their own tests.

This disease, which occurs in all parts of the world, is caused by a microscopic organism, Salmonella pullorum. The chicken seems to be the natural host of the organism. The main reservoirs of pullorum infection are the egg-producing organs of the infected female. The disease is transmitted from her to her young directly through the egg. Pullorum disease may also strike turkeys, ducks, guinea fowl, pheasants, sparrows, quail, geese, pigeons, doves, parakeets, and canaries. The organism, which was discovered in 1899, is rarely found in mammals. Once commonly known as bacillary white diarrhea (BWD) of chicks, pullorum disease has been recognized for more than half a century as one of the worst of all poultry diseases.

Pullorum disease causes heavy death losses in chicks and poults and reduces the productivity of adult birds. The deaths occur mainly during the first three weeks after hatching. Losses may be as high as 80-90 per cent of the brood. Pullorum disease is not commonly encountered in the acute form in birds more than one month old. Infected adults usually show no outward evidence of infection.

Great strides have been made toward eradicating pullorum through the national program of blood testing adult breeding flocks, supplemented with sound sanitation. The infection may be spread amount the brood though breathing or consuming contaminated dust, down, or other material in the incubator, shipping box, brooder, or pen. The disease is also transmitted through consumption of litter, fed, or water contaminated with infected droppings. One infected chick or poult at hatching time may be responsible for transmitting the disease to the entire brood. The infection is usually spread during the firs few days.

Unsanitary conditions, improper heating or ventilation, and the occurrence of other dise3ases can hasten spread. Infected chicks or poults that do not die of the disease may grow to maturity and remain lifetime carriers. Infected hens may lay infected eggs that may hatch diseased chicks; thus, the cycle is repeated.

Control and Eradication of Pullorum

Pullorum disease control must be based on breaking the cycle of transmission. This id done by detecting and eliminating adult carriers, because the disease is largely egg borne. Such a procedure makes the owner reasonable sure that only non-infected eggs are set and non-infected chicks and poults are hatched.

Blood-testing of adult chickens and turkeys in breeding flocks is done throughout the United States. The agglutination test, used in detecting pullorum carriers, is conducted by one or more of the four officially recognized methods, namely, the agglutination test, the rapid whole-blood plate test, the rapid serum plate-test and the micro-agglutination test. Each test is based on the fact that infected birds carry in their blood stream immune substances (antibodies), which will clump (stick together or agglutinate) a liquid suspension of killed-pullorum organisms (antigens) when the test suspension is mixed with the serum or the whole blood of the infected bird. The blood of non-infected birds does not contain pullorum antibodies, and therefore no clump form when the whole blood or serum of such birds is mixed with the antigen.

A pullorum-testing program is mandatory in many states. Some states require complete flock-testing of foundation breeders of chickens, turkeys, fancier show birds, guinea fowl, and other susceptible species. A negative pullorum test or certification that birds originated from pullorum-clean flocks is required by most states for birds being exhibited at shows and fairs. Such requirements have been helpful in locating pullorum-infected flocks of hobby, fancy, or exhibition chickens, thereby bringing the nation a step closer to being free of pullorum.

Fowl Typhoid Disease and other Diseases

Fowl Typhoid is caused by another salmonella closely related to pullorum, and two diseases share common antigens. Birds infected with fowl typhoid react to the pullorum test. Fowl typhoid has been considered on the same basis as pullorum by NPIP since 1954. That is the reason why poultry flocks with a negative test are now designated as "U.S. Pullorum and Typhoid Free".

Tests are also used to identify and eradicate other egg-transmitted diseases in the breeding and hatching of commercial poultry. Several types of Mycoplasma are being identified and eliminated through this process. Egg-transmitted or hatchery-transmitted bacterial diseases that my be controlled by management programs or where the infected breeding flock may be identified by diagnostic tests may lend themselves to future National Plan Programs!

Where To Get More Information!

Each year, the National Poultry Improvement Plan staff publishes a list of breeders and hatcheries that participate in the program. Copies of these list are available by writing to:
>Poultry Improvement Plan
>APHIS_VS
>U.S. Dept. of Agriculture
>Building 265, BARC-East
>Beltsville, MD 20705

Included with the lists are the names and addresses of the official State agencies. These state agencies are the organizations to contact if you are interested in participating the NPIP.

Pullorum Disease of Chickens & Turkeys (Uncontrolled * Controlled)

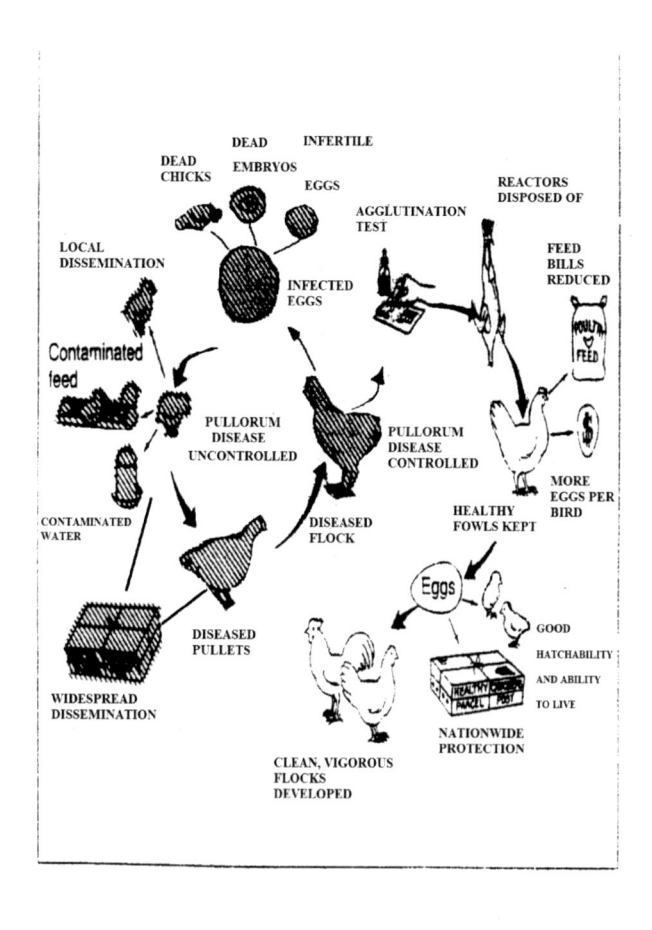

Stress

Stress is one of the leading causes of death with gamebirds. Some factors causing stress are as follows:

1. ILLNESS

2. MOVING BIRDS FROM ONE PEN TO ANOTHER.

3. PUTTING TOO MANY BIRDS IN A BROODER OR PEN.

4. CATCHING AND HANDLING BIRDS FOR ANY REASON

5. WEATHER CHANGES.

6. BEING FRIGHTENED BY PREDATORS

7. SHIPPING.

During times of stress, the addition of a stress pack, an electrolyte mixture, or an antibiotic such as terramyacin will help the birds maintain their normal body functions.

Handling

Don't injure or cause the death of birds by mishandling them. Never grab any bird by its legs. Gently clasp the hands over the wings, draw the bird against your body, and then get hold of its legs.

<u>Signs Of Illness</u>

1. Decreased or increased food and water consumption.

2. Increased sleeping, decreased movements about pen or cage, lack of response to external stimulus.

3. Ruffled feathers, hunched-up posture, or drooping wings.

4. Inability to stand or sits low on roost.

5. Heavy or open-mouthed breathing.

6. Abnormal clicking, wheezing or sneezing.

7. Drop in weight or general body condition (A prominent breast bone is a sign of a really sick bird.)

8. Discharge of the eyes, nostrils, or mouth (Look for discolored feathers.)

9. Change in the droppings.

10. Enlargement or swellings.

11. Vomiting or regurgitation.

Guineas

The Watchdog of the Barnyard

The Guinea is a native of Africa and derive their name from a section of the west coast of Africa. They have been domesticated since the days of ancient Greece. The common domestic Guinea fowl descended from one of the wild African species and comes in several distinct colors: Lavender - Blue - Pearl. The Pearl Guinea is usually the most popular today.

This very different gamebird is fast becoming known for its ability to eat a lot of bugs and ticks in the garden and protect the farm from intruders.

Domestic guineas have a tendency to cling to the wild habits and are sometimes considered hard to raise for that reason. This is because they will hide their nests, and will refuse to incubate their eggs if their nests becomes disturbed by any intruders. If left undisturbed throughout their setting time they can hatch as many as 30 or more eggs. The incubation time for a guinea is 28 days and is raised much the same as the pheasant. Guineas' are actually in the pheasant family. It is a hardy bird and when dressed tastes much the same as a pheasant, usually weighing about 3 lbs. average at 16 to 18 weeks of age.

It is difficult to sex domestic Guinea fowl because the plumage is identical for both the male and the female. The male has a larger, coarser looking head and the red wattles are longer and have thicker edges. When startled, the hen can emit a shrill one syllable shriek similar to that made by the male, but the hen usually makes a two-syllable call that sound like "Put-rock, "Put-rock."

JungleFowl

Junglefowl, any of several wild pheasant like birds that include the ancestor of the domestic fowl. The chicken, Gallus gallus or G. domesticus, is a domestic fowl, probably the most common bird in the world. It is raised for meat, eggs, and by-products such as feathers; for sport; and as a hobby. It was developed chiefly from the Red Junglefowl ((Gallus)) found throughout Southeast Asia and some Pacific Islands. In the wild they inhabit woodlands and bushy fields from sea level to altitudes of about 5000 feet (1500 meters). Junglefowl generally travel in flocks and, when disturbed, call noisily. They feed on seeds, plants, and insects. In captivity they feed well on any gamebird or gamecock feed.

The best-known species is the Red Junglefowl (Gallus Gallus Murghi), which is found throughout the Far East. The male resembles a fighting cock. It has a long, high-arched tail, twin-wattles throat, and saw-toothed frontal comb. Its' head-to-tail length is about 32 inches. The body feathers are mostly shades of yellow and brown, and the tail is greenish black. The female Junglefowl is considerably smaller and brownish.

In captivity they are very easy to raise. When raised in ground pens they will burrow a hole in the ground to bury their eggs before setting the. Quite often it is like an Easter egg hunt to find them. We always incubate them, but of course they are quite good mothers and will set, hatch and raise their young. The incubation time is 21 days.

When brooding Junglefowl you would use the same methods as with any gamebird. A good schedule to use is the one we use for the quail etc. Read about this in the section devoted to the Bobwhite quail.

The Ringneck Pheasant

These colorful fowl larger in size than their relatives the partridge and quail fly at great speed for short distances due to their typically short wings. Though most are good walkers and spend much time on the ground scratching and digging for food.

Their ornamental plumage of the males makes these birds much different from their family members the partridge and quail; greens, browns, blues, reds, yellows, black, white and slate in various combinations of bold or complicated patterns are often accentuated by a cape, crest, wattle, or elongate train.

The Ringneck Pheasant was introduced into the U.S. successfully in 1880. They have become widespread and important as a gamebird on the farm lands of the northern half of the continental U.S. and extreme Southern Canada.

When rearing baby pheasants we use much the same methods as for other gamebirds. (Refer to brooding instructions for quail.) They, like bobwhites must be encouraged to eat and offering them hard boiled eggs ground is a good practice for the first few days of their life.

Once they have left the brooder stage and are ready to go outside be sure you don't make the mistake of over crowding your birds. At least 5 square feet of pen space should be provided for each 6 week old pheasant. Pheasants do best out on the ground and they must have adequate pen space to hold down cannibalism.

Feather picking is a serious problem that can be caused by numerous factors including improper diet, crowding, and brooding aggressive chicks. As often as you can give them raw tomatoes. This is nutritious for them and discourages pecking. When they reach the age of about eight weeks old you can use poly peepers or bits. Debeaking is also recommended, although this will have to be repeated before they are grown.

Pheasants must have larger pens as they reach their full maturity. This can vary with the amount of vegetation in the pen. In fact, a rotation of pens, providing new forage as the birds grow is a most excellent program. We usually keep one cock to five hens.

Hint:: **If pheasants, partridge, and quail are kept on the ground build their pens on slightly sloping ground with good drainage. If water stands in the pens, there is a greater potential for increased outbreaks of disease.**

Cannibalism can be traced to one of three things:

1. **Overcrowding**
2. **Insufficient protein in feed**
3. **Insufficient greens for them to peck at.**

Don't overcrowd birds in the brooder or pen. Provide plenty of feeders and wateriers and never let them get empty. Avoid bright light and over-heating as these factors can also trigger cannibalism. Provide birds with roosts, brush piles, tall grass, etc. where they can escape when they are being pecked. Divert the attention of the birds to pecking on greens such as lettuce, lamb quarter, dandelions, or grass clippings.

If first year hatched pheasants and chukars are not well feathered out, it could be due to the fact that the birds are picking at each others feathers. Feather-picking can result from placing too many birds into a pen. A change in diet usually does not correct this habit once it is started. Bits, specs, or peepers are fairly effective in preventing feather pecking. Measures should be taken now to help birds develop feathers which will help them to survive the cold this winter.

Disease can be a very severe problem, especially in large flocks of birds. Of course, the best cure is prevention of which the main factors are good feed, adequate pen space and good sanitation and maintenance.

Calcium For Breeder Birds

Everyone knows that a laying hen requires a steady intake of calcium. The hen must be able to wrap in the egg all the nutrients needed by the embryo for developing and hatching. The hen wraps the nutrients in the egg-shell. To produce good egg shells, the hen requires proper calcium   The cock and hen have different calcium requirements. The rooster doesn't have to produce egg-shells. This is why you should let the hen obtain extra calcium "free choice", as a supplement of oyster shell or grit.

Birds in high egg production risk egg binding and general exhaustion if their diet is not complete in all essential vitamins and minerals and formulated to supply an increased supply of protein, calcium and energy (calories).).

IMPORTANT TO KNOW!

You can save a lot of money on your feed costs if you will be sure not to overfeed your birds. The only time you need "deep feed" in your feeders is when the

The birds are severely debeaked. Research shows that you'll improve the growth and livability of your birds if feed troughs aren't over-filled. Maintaining too much feed in feeders allows "fines", moisture and fungi to build up the feeders also.

ALWAYS **take advantage of the professional advice and help that is available to you. If you know all that you can about your birds you will be able to effectively prevent, control and treat any diseases that could arise. The most can be learned about your birds by simple intelligent observations. Take time out to do this and each time you will learn more to be able to detect normal behavior from abnormal behavior. Train yourself to detect and anticipate problems and diseases before they become tragedies!!**

Hint: Newly hatched chicks often encounter stress because of improper brooding temperatures and over-crowding.

The Chukar Partridge

The Chukar is a medium sized gamebird of the pheasant family also known as the partridge. The word partridge is often applied to quail as well. The Chukar has unfettered legs and exposed nostrils unlike its close relative the grouse.

Eating a quantity of insects, waste grain, and weed seeds, this gray partridge is most at home in its' native land of Europe and Asia, though in large numbers was introduced into the United States and Canada and is well established. It was introduced into California in the early 1930s to help the state supply birds for hunting and recreation. The neck and upper breast are gray, the back is brown streaked with buff on the face and sides of the head are buff also. The sides of the body are banded with gray and reddish yellow, and on the lower side of the body is a horsehoe shaped area that is usually dark chestnut.

In setting Chukar eggs, the eggs should be set at 99.5 F. and a wet bulb temperature of 86 F. Eggs should be placed small end down and turned 90 F. three times a day. On the 21st day the eggs should be placed on their sides in the hatcher. The hatcher should be set at 99 F. with a wet bulb reading 87 F. Around the 23rd day eggs should hatch. If eggs are to be held any length of time before they are set, they should be kept small end down, turned three times a day, and at a temperature between 60-68 F. Always be sure your hands are free of dirt and grease when handling eggs.

Chukars are known for piling a corner of their pen and smothering eachother. Birds pile because they are scared or because they are cold. In an attempt to keep warm, they huddle together and those on the bottom are smothered. You should maintain the proper brooder temperature so that the chicks will bed down in a ring near the source of heat. If the nights turn cold just after putting older birds outside, try turning on a light or two to lessen the chances of them piling up in corners of the pen.

Young chukars between the ages of two to ten weeks are very susceptible to coccidiosis. Warmth and moisture are conditions which are necessary for the development of the parasite eggs which are found in the droppings of infected chukars. It is best to raise young chukars away from older chukars and in pens having wire floors. (Refer to disease section.) Amprol and Sulmet can be used in drinking water for treating coccidiosis.

If chukar partridge between the ages of eight to sixteen weeks are raised no t he ground, they re highly susceptible to blackhead. The primary source of the disease is their ingestion of the cecal worms which are which are infected with the blackhead organism.

Maintaining good sanitation, controlling cecal worms, and rearing chukars away from chickens or off an area that has been used previously by chickens is extremely important. Many breeders use NF180 or Furazolidone for the prevention of blackhead. If birds are raised on wire, worming the birds when they are four of five weeks of age and again when they are eight or nine weeks old will reduce or completely rid them of cecal worms. Water soluble Tramisol is effective against cecal worms. Normal disease control practices should be used.

We have found that the Chukar is capable of breeding in pairs well as in trio's and colonies with the same amount of fertility rate while in captivity. Although same amount of fertility rate while in captivity. Although in the wild they are only know to be monogamous. We feel all three methods are productive. The Chukar is an easy bird to raise and produces abundantly given the correct methods are practiced with care, good sanitation and maintenance.

FASTRACK For All Your Animals!

LIVESTOCK

GAMEBIRDS

DOMESTIC PETS

74

If You Have Your Health

Everything depends on good health. This is true for you and your animals. Medical science has long known that people who eat cultured dairy products have less digestive problems. This is because just one ounce of yogurt or milk with sweet acidophilus contains several hundred million beneficial bacteria. These bacteria can cure colitis, and also diarrhea caused by antibiotics. All of us have experienced the effects of stress in our lives. We know from experience that stress causes acids to flow in our digestive tract and can lead to digestive upset, especially when we travel and eat different foods and drink exotic beverages. And, we all take steps to prevent digestive problems.

Animals under stress suffer the same problems, but it is up to you to manage the problems. The concept of feeding large amounts of beneficial microbes to combat the negative effect of stress has been proven in the commercial livestock and ratite industry. We have proven it to work as well in the gamebird industry.

Shipping, new environments, feed changes, weaning, weather change's crowding and antibiotic therapy can adversely affect the balance of normal populations of gut microflora. This results in diarrhea, gastroenteritis, reduced feed intake or even death.

The use of direct-fed, specific microbials may increase an animal's ability to produce anti-bacterial compounds, and create conditions compatible with pathogen grown, (compete for space and/or nutrients), produce digestive enzymes, stimulate immune response and/or detoxify pathogenic toxins.

It makes sense, the use of specific beneficial bacteria can help maintain a healthy state in your animals digestive tracks, and will encourage appetites even during severe changes. This is true for all creatures large and small. Microbials are a management tool that may have a beneficial impact for the majority of creatures in the gamebird and exotic world.

The performance and health of your gamebirds is dependent upon the proper balance of digestive tract bacteria. Newly-hatched birds enter the world with a sterile digestive tract, which is quickly populated with health-promoting bacteria and the much quicker growing, pathogenic bacteria and viruses. Unfortunately, feed and environmental changes, hatching/laying, medication and transporting, among other common management practices alter the intestinal environment in ways that favor the disease-causing organisms of birds of any age.

Fastrack is for all your animals -large and small! READ ON!!!!!!!!!!!!!!!!!!

Protect Your Investments
With *FASTRACK*MICRO FEEDS*

You're in business to make money! Adding Fastrack's unique direct-fed microbials costs pennies a day and feed your bottom-line profits!

Naturally complements the digestive system: Fastrack probiotics contain a source of live (viable) natural occurring micro-organisms.

A Fastrack Feed for every need: Perfect for newborn animals, at weaning, at shipping, after antibiotic therapy. Maintains appetite during periods of stress and stimulates the immune system.

Completely safe and easy to use: Contains live lactic acid bacteria, live yeast and products rich in vitamins and enzymes. Available in easy to use oral paste or gel, as a top dressing for feeds and as liquid dispersible crystals for water or milk replacers.

Find out for yourself Fastrack works: You'll wonder how you got along without it!!

Probiotic Means "For Life"

1. Aids in digestion (good stools)
2. Inhibit disease causing bacteria
3. Increases birds activity and lowers stress, reduces mortality.
4. Increases egg production, making a healthier bird.

Predator Control

When raising gamebirds it is essential to have a good basic knowledge of the types of predators you may encounter. It can be a very serious financial blow to have your gamebirds needlessly killed by predators out of control.

The best way to protect your gamebirds from predators is of course to practice preventive control by building strong, enclosed, and well covered cages and flight pens. Although even if you build your pens so that a predator cannot gain immediate access from the outside they can still do a lot of damage by stressing the birds while trying to get in. If you can build a barrier at least two feet above the bottom all around a flight pen area it will help to keep this from happening.

Common Predators Are:

1. **SKUNKS.** They are the number one carrier of rabies. We are all offended by their foul odor. They usually single out a victim and are very clumsy killers.

2. **RACCOONS.** This is a very intelligent, strong, relentless killer. He can climb and tear wire or netting. They kill large numbers at a time leaving them in piles. They prefer to eat the area from the head to the breast.

3. **OPOSSUM.** They are able to climb and tear open pens. They maul their victims and have a taste for the eggs also.

4. **GREAT HORNED OWLS.** are cunning, powerful and efficient killers. They dive a flight pen to catch their victims in the top of the netting and usually decapitate them, killing several in one night. Flashing red lights can deter them.

5 **HAWKS** will kill several birds at a time. It feeds on most of the carcass, accept for the gizzard and feathers.

6 **SNAKES.** It will consume most smaller gamebirds, such as the quail - chicks and grown . When visiting pheasant or chukar areas they usually target the eggs.

Internal Parasites

Cecal Worms are eaten by earthworms, which in turn is ingested by the gamebird to become infected with histomoniasis (blackhead). This is why Chukars and Turkeys are best reared up on wire. They are the most susceptible to this parasite.

Gapeworms infects the trachea (windpipe) of pheasants and turkeys. It can be a very serious problem with pheasant. Usually young birds are more susceptible. The birds will have the following symptoms when infected with these worms.

- Eye closed and head drawn back
- Time to time they throw their head forward and upward and open their mouths to draw in air
- Sometimes can have convulsive shakes
- General weakness and a emaciated appearance

Capillary Worms commonly infect the crop and esophagus. Eggs of this parasite will be passed in the droppings of the infected birds. They can become infected with this worm by swallowing infected earthworms.

Symptoms are primarily:

- Malnutrition
- Emaciation
- Severe anemia

When infestation becomes too severe there is no medication that will be very effective when it comes to infestation of worms. Preventive medicine practices is the best method of control.

The following are some good practices to keep in force:

- Rearing gamebirds on wire.

- Keep birds on a schedules deworming program.

- Pen rotation with cultivation of soil for ground pens.

- Keep pens well drained.

- After each rotation fumigate the pen with something that is not harmful to birds. (such as clorox)

- Tramisol is effective against all worm species.

Egg Binding

Egg binding is a common reproductive problem that causes the bird to retain the egg in the reproductive tract, unable to expel it naturally. Female budgerigars, cockatiels, lovebirds, large parrots, and overweight birds commonly suffer from egg binding.

Symptoms and Types

A bird suffering from egg binding will have a swollen abdomen and wag its tail frequently. The bird will also have difficulty balancing on the perch. And its leg may be paralyzed, if the egg presses on a nerve it can give it a lot of pain.

Causes

Egg binding is caused by the inability to expel an egg naturally, and is generally due to a deficiency of calcium in the bird's diet.

Treatment

Do not attempt to remove the egg yourself, as you can cause the bird harm – paralysis or death. Instead, take the bird to a veterinarian. X-rays will be taken to locate the egg and check for any abnormality in egg size. Afterwards, the veterinarian may try natural expulsion of the egg: giving the bird calcium, humid environment, lots of fluids, warmth and lubrication of the passage. They may also inject female hormones like oxytocin and prostaglandin to help the bird expel the egg. If all the previous methods fail, the veterinarian will extract the egg by hand or surgically.

Avian Influenza

Avian influenza (or bird flu) is a lung and airway disease found in birds, and it is caused by the influenza virus. This viral infection can also spread to humans, so if your bird is infected, seek immediate treatment and take all necessary precautions to prevent an outbreak of bird flu.

Because of its infectious potential to humans, any breakout of avian influenza has to be reported to Center for Disease Control and Prevention (CDC) in the United States. Recently, a ban has been placed on imported pet birds from countries where bird flu has been reported (i.e., certain African, Asian and European countries).

(MESH POULTRY NETTING - USE PLASTIC ON OUTSIDE DURING COLD WEATHER)

PERSPECTIVE

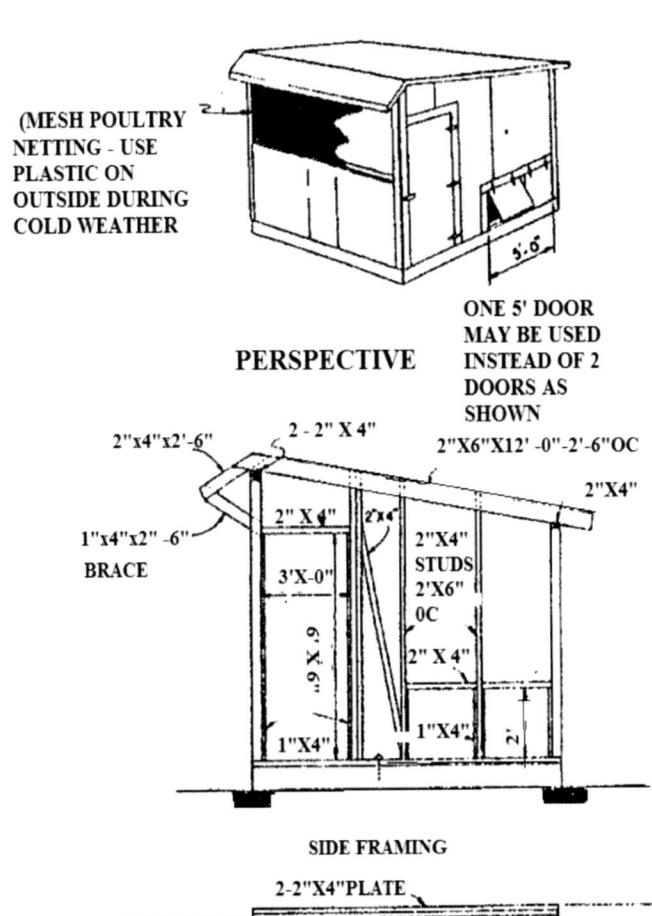

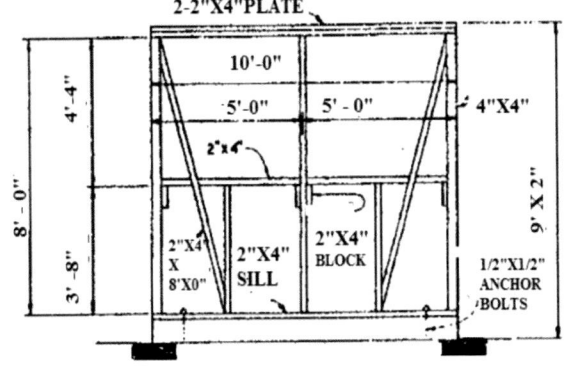

ONE 5' DOOR MAY BE USED INSTEAD OF 2 DOORS AS SHOWN

2"x4"x2'-6"
2 - 2" X 4"
2"X6"X12'-0"-2'-6"OC
2"X4"
1"x4"x2'-6" BRACE
2" X 4"
2"x4"
2"X4" STUDS 2"X6" OC
3'X-0"
9' X 6"
2" X 4"
1"X4"
1"X4"
2'

SIDE FRAMING

2-2"X4"PLATE
10'-0"
4'-4"
5'-0"   5'-0"
4"X4"
2"x4"
8'-0"
9' X 2"
3'-8"
2"X4" X 8'X0"
2"X4" SILL
2"X4" BLOCK
1/2"X1/2" ANCHOR BOLTS

FRONT FRAMING

83

PLAN

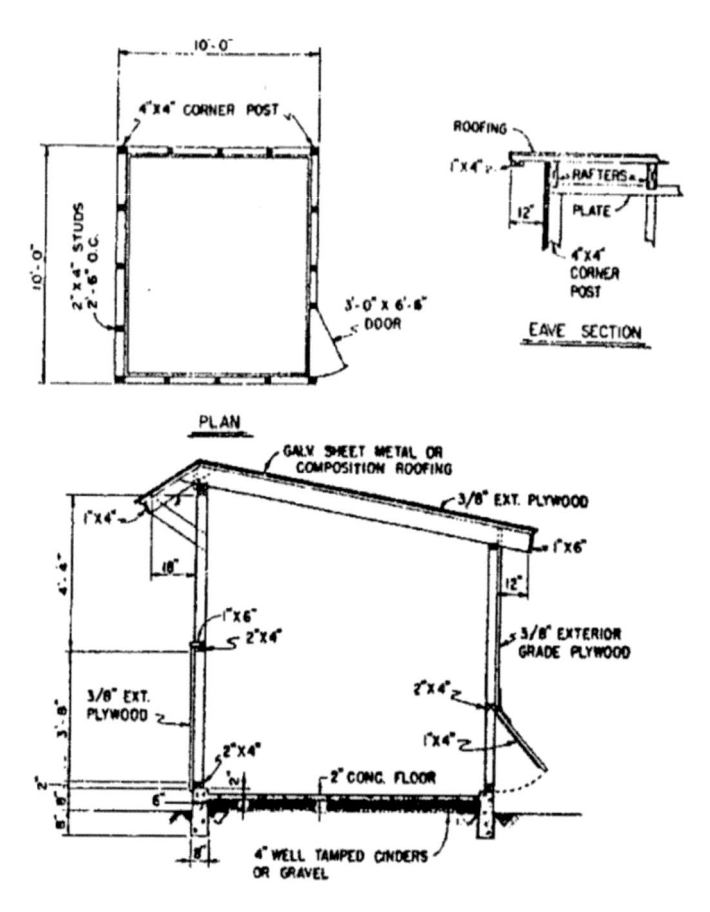

EAVE SECTION

CROSS SECTION

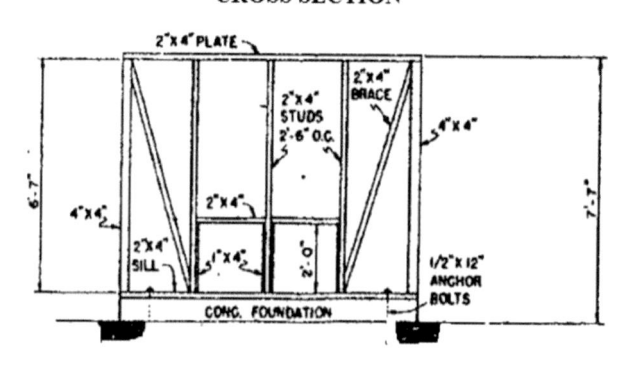

REAR FRAMING

BROODER   **SUN PORCH**

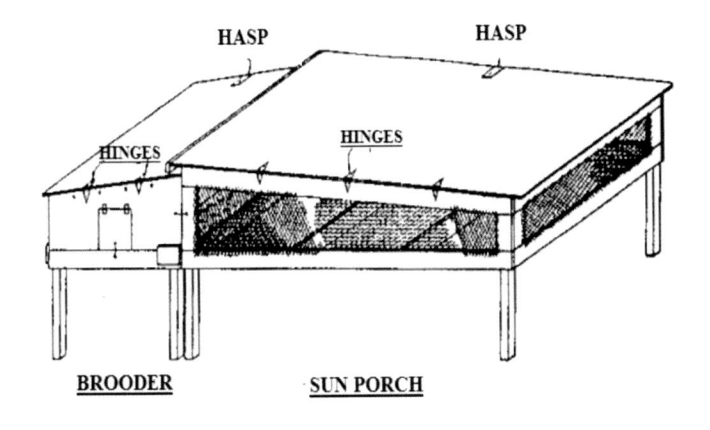

PERSPECTIVE

MATERIALS - BROODER

1 sheet 4'x8'x3/8" exterior grade plywood
1 - 1" x 2" x 6'
4 - 1" x 4" x 10'
1 - 2" x 2" x 10'
1 pr. small hinges
1 lb. 6penny nails
1/2 lb. 8 penny nails
4 lin.ft. 1/2" or 3/4" mesh hardware colot 3ft.
Drop curtain 7' x 48"
3 large screen doors hooks and eyes

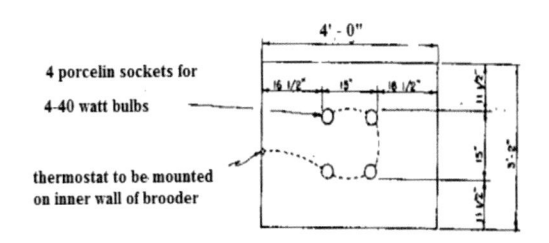

4 porcelin sockets for
4-40 watt bulbs

thermostat to be mounted
on inner wall of brooder

ELECTRICAL LAYOUT FOR BROODER

85

PLANS FOR OUTDOOR ELECTRIC BROODER

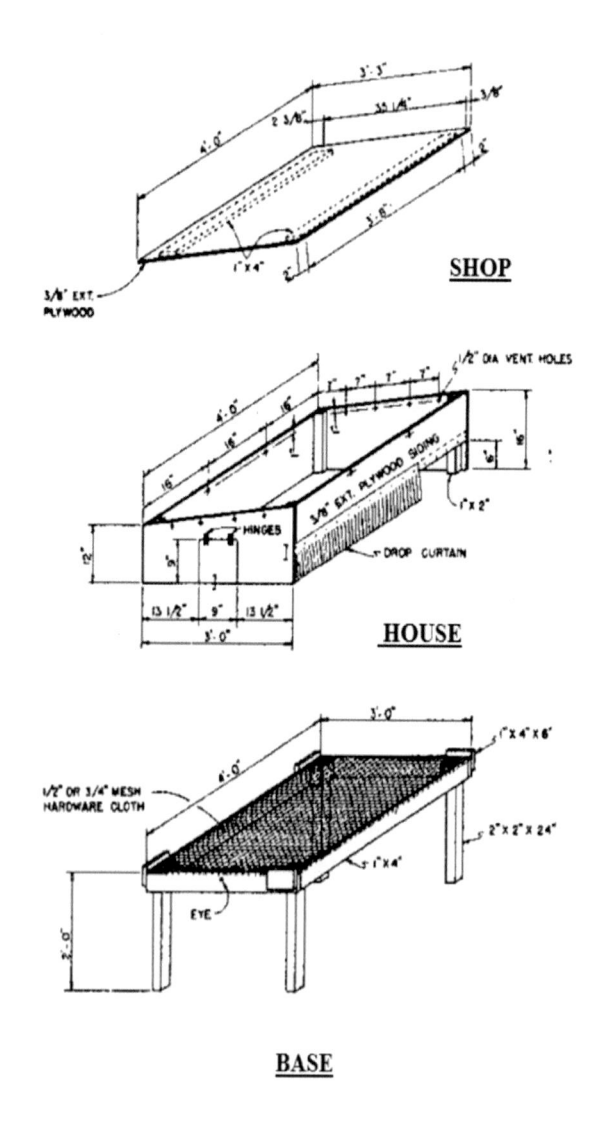

SHOP

HOUSE

BASE

BILL OF MATERIALS
SUN PORCH
10 1" X 4" X 8'
20 LIN.FT. 1" MESH POULTRY WIRE 3' WIDE
1/2" OR 3/4" HARDWARE CLOTH 3' WIDE
2 - 2" X 2" X 8'
1/2 LB. 6 PENNY NAILS
1/2 LB. 8 PENNY NAILS
1 LB. WIRE STAPLES
1 - 4' X 8' X 3/8" EXTERIOR GRADE PLYWOOD
1 - 1" X 2" X 4'

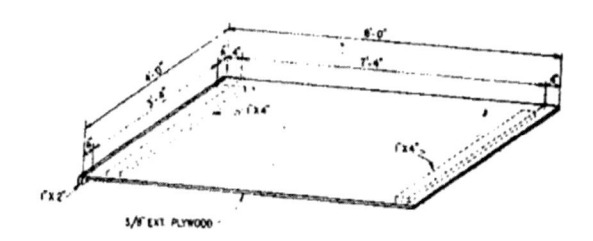

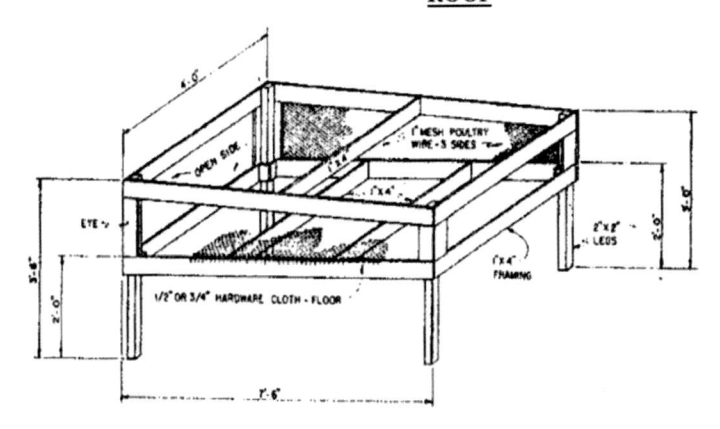

ROOF

SUN PORCH

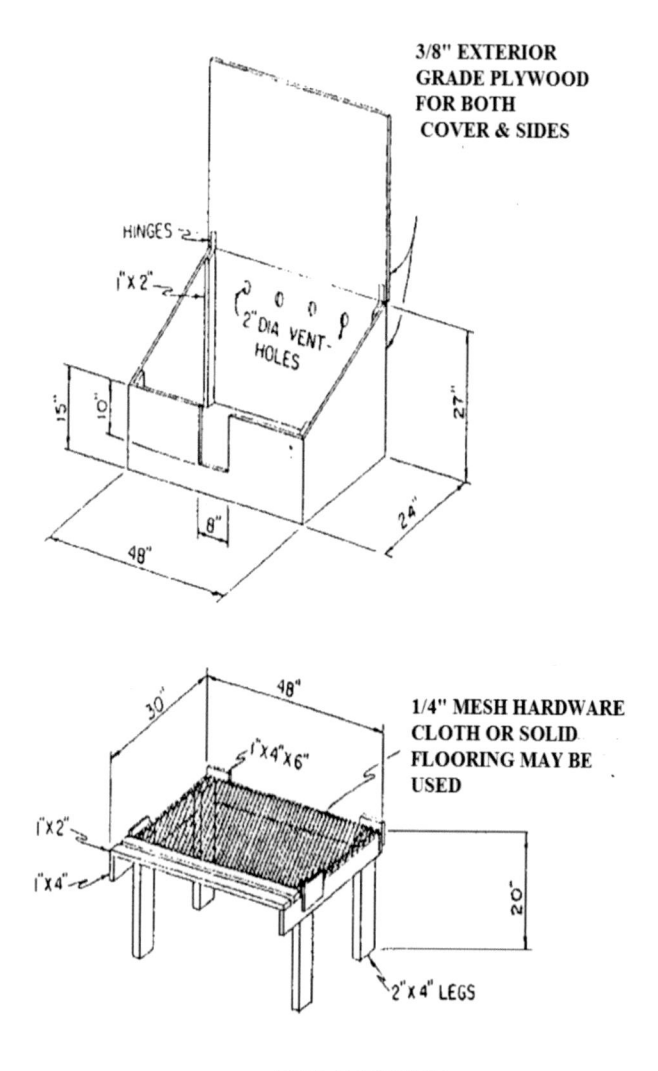

COMMUNITY NEST

100 FT. QUAIL FLIGHT PENS

Associations

North American Gamebird Association

Brian Beavers, NAGA Treasurer/Webmaster

01406 E. Hwy 50, Pierceville, KS 67868

Phone: (620) 335-5405 info@mynaga.org

National Wildlife Association

Department of Wildlife

1801 N. Lincoln

P.O. Box 53465, OKC., OK 73152

Oklahoma Wildlife Federation

4545 Lincoln Blvd. Suite 171

Okla. City, OK 73105

Quail Unlimited

National Headquarters

P.O. Box 10041, Augusta, GA 30903

Oklahoma Wildlife Federation

4545 Lincoln Blvd. Suite 171

Okla. City, OK 73105

Quail Unlimited

National Headquarters

P.O. Box 10041, Augusta, GA 30903

American Game Bird Breeders

The Gazette

1155 E. 4780 South

Salt Lake City, Utah 84117

Heart of America

Rt. 1 Box 20, Bucyrus, Kansas 66013

American Poultry Association

26363 S. Tucker Road, Estacada, Oregon 97023

Sources Of Equipment

B & D Game Farm

332939 East 1020 Rd.

Harrah, OK 73045   (405)964-5235/

(biddie drinkers, waterers, feeders, poly peepers, shipping crates, egg shipping containers, books and videos.)

E-Mail: bdfarm@mcloudteleco.com

Website: www.bdfarm.com

Randall Burkey Co., Inc.

117 Industrial Drive

Boerne, TX 78006   (800)531-1097

(brooders, feeders, general equipment.)

GQF Mfg. Co.

P.O. Box 1552

Savannah, Georgia 31402   (912)236-0651

(gamebird eggs, brooders, feeders, general equipment)

Kuhl Corporation

Kuhl Road P.O. Box 26

Flemington, New Jersey 08822   (908)782-5696

(incubators, cages, processing equipment, crates)

Cutlers' Supply Co.

3805 Washington road

Carsonville, Michigan 48419   (810)657-9450

(brooders, feeders, netting, incubators, gamebird supplies) Website: www.cutlersupply.com

Jeffers Supply

P.O. Box 948

West Plains, MO 65775-0948   (800)533-3377

(pet, gamebird, equine and other supplies.)

Important Phone Numbers

Medication Records

FACTS

ON

RAISING

GAMEBIRDS

COPYRIGHT   1988 BY Dianne Tumey

All Rights Reserved.

1st Edition Jan. 1987

2nd Edition April 1990

3rd Edition Feb. 1993

4th Edition Dec. 1996

5th Edition April 2014

No portion of this book may be reproduced in any way without the written permission of the publisher, except for brief excerpts in reviews, etc.

Printed in Harrah, OK USA

This book is available to dealers, retailers, libraries and bird clubs in wholesale quantities.

DianneTumey 332939 East 1020 Rd Harrah, OK 73045 (405)964-5235

Dianne Tumey...…………………......Art Work,Photos

Marcine Jackson..…………………………….....Photos

LARGE NORTHERN BOBWHITE

CORTURNIX (PHAROAH D1) QUAIL

TIBETAN QUAIL

EASTERN WILD TURKEY

GUINEA FOWL

RINGNECK PHEASANT (COCK)

PHAROAH XLD1 DAY-OLD CHICK

TENNESSEE RED BOBWHITE QUAIL

CHUKAR PARTRIDGE

JUNGLEFOWL (INDIAN RED)

Made in the USA
Columbia, SC
11 June 2019